# LONDON
# PECULIARS

# LONDON PECULIARS

## A GUIDE TO THE CITY'S OFFBEAT PLACES

Peter Ashley

ACC ART BOOKS

# INTRODUCTION

**Opposite:** A glance down Carmelite Street revealed a regal wave from the other side of the Thames. This was a photographic mural placed on Sea Containers House to celebrate The Queen's Diamond Jubilee in 2012. Taken by an unknown photographer at Buckingham Palace in 1977, it became the largest ever photo of the Royal Family
**Previous spread:**
**Far left:** The coffee bean grinder sign at Berry Bros. & Rudd. See page 48
**Left:** An architectural trademark transformed into bridge guardian. See page 18
**Right:** Virtually redundant, the line-up of telephone boxes in Carey Street at the rear of the Law Courts on the Strand
**Far right:** The contents of this cast-iron channel above the platforms of Sloane Square Underground station is the River Westbourne, now mainly invisible except for where it decants into the Thames at Chelsea

Knowing my predilection for these things, I was once asked by English Heritage to take photographs and write books about curiosities in the capital city. I decided to call the subject *London Peculiars*, getting mixed up with London Particulars, which are, of course, dense fogs obscuring everything.

Peculiars they became, in the sense of "having eccentric or individual variations to the general or predicted pattern", although a great many did indeed emerge from their past as if a fog had cleared to reveal them. This handbook is a much more manageable and completely revised version of the two originals, taking the best of both and adding more Peculiars that have subsequently manifested themselves.

These things have a much wider audience now, thanks to the instant gratification of the internet. But I can look back and remember the diverse ways I came to learn of these Peculiars, and indeed still do. Sometimes they were the result of a pub conversation, sometimes even overhearing things like "Have you seen those dummy house fronts in Bayswater?" As Iain Sinclair said in his essay 'Bright Lights on Ordinary Ghosts' that prefaced my first volume: "He listens to rumours in pubs and he runs those rumours to ground".

Rumours became fact; unexpected discoveries were found in hidden corners; friendly cab drivers pointed down alleyways.

A baroque Thames embarkation point marooned in a public park 300 feet from the river; council flat railings made from ARP wartime stretchers that I was told were an urban myth, until I found them for myself; a lion asleep on the tomb of a sadistic menagerist in a

'Victorian Valhalla' on a Highgate hillside; and the fading remnants of long-lost lettering, still exhorting their forgotten messages… all are so typical of the continual ebb and flow of London life, the buildings and objects that have moved around this city in mysterious ways.

I also had a brilliant leg-up from someone who had already been out on the streets back in the 1940s. Peter Jackson drew cartoon strips for *The Evening News*, which presented eclectic, fascinating and preposterous facts about London in superb line drawings. The panels were collected into at least two books – *London Is Stranger Than Fiction* and *London Explorer* – and one dark winter's afternoon in the late 1980s I had the luck to find them in an appropriately dimly-lit junk shop in Deptford. Some of the entries smacked of Mr. Jackson also making notes late at night in noisy pubs, like hearing of the Edmonton hen that laid an egg with an inscription on it that warned of an imminent earthquake. Mostly though, his was a catalogue of genuine oddities that he collected, magpie-like, from his Kensington studio. Naturally, much has changed since the 1940s.

Of course, treasures like these can't just be copied slavishly from other people's endeavours. One of the most rewarding aspects of collecting Peculiars is discovering things for one's self. So many times I saw something, thought about it, photographed it and then found out about it. And when friends realised what I was doing, I was immediately offered more candidates. This way I discovered a chimney on the Greenwich Peninsula that confirmed the fact that such edifices are not always from London's remote past. Like alien spacecraft that send out signals, London leaves a trail of clues for the inquisitive among us to follow. In the years since my first wanderings, a few Peculiars have receded somewhat, like the car distributors' sign in Twickenham, which has since been overpainted. However, I feel they should still be recorded.

As a handbook, *London Peculiars* should fit snugly into a bag, capacious pocket or glove box, and all you will need in addition is a street atlas, an up-to-date Underground map and a stout pair of shoes. Most Peculiars are within the central area, but all should be easily accessible. And of course, hopefully you will find curiosities of your own.

"... IN YOUR QUEST FOR RECONNECTING ONE MAN'S COLLECTION OF URBAN ODDITIES, YOU WILL CREATE YOUR OWN NARRATIVE AND SEE LONDON AS IT IS, THE MOST BAROQUE OF FICTIONS. AN ATLAS OF POTENTIALITIES. AN UNAUTHORED NOVEL."

- Iain Sinclair

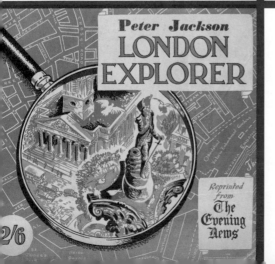

# LONDON
# CREATURES

# THE CRYSTAL PALACE PREHISTORIC MENAGERIE

**THICKET ROAD, SYDENHAM ⇌ CRYSTAL PALACE**

**Below:** Megalosaurus. Designed and sculpted by Benjamin Waterhouse Hawkins
**Previous spread:** "Double chips, please." The fish that once announced a restaurant

Restored, painted and given fresh ferns to tear away at are the original prehistoric animals that were placed on this Sydenham hillside when the Crystal Palace was re-assembled here in 1852. The mastodon was so big that the Victorians did what they always did when confronted by something large and exciting: 21 of them sat down inside it to have dinner.

Together with a few newer friends, they line the water's edge of a small lake surrounded by thoughtfully placed paths, which facilitate good views of them munching and silently roaring up into the trees. I imagine that most people bringing their children here don't realise that the originals are over 150 years old, and not some *Jurassic Park* spin-off to feed the current dinosaur craze. These pale green creatures with their baleful lizard eyes are an intriguing remembrance of what once stood here on one of London's highest points, a site that still mourns the extinction of another dinosaur, the Crystal Palace.

# 222 STRAND

**Below:** The astounding vestibule of
222 Strand

Whilst photographing the Royal Courts of Justice on the Strand, I inadvertently stepped backwards and found a slimy flying fish staring at me as it flapped down a tiled wall. I was in the vestibule of the Law Courts branch of Lloyds, and looking around I was confronted by a highly polished display of Doulton ware decorative tiles and mosaics. Designed and painted by John H. McLennan, the majolica subjects include the grotesque fish, lions' heads, acanthus leaves and curious half-naked men flexing their muscles. It's a mix of Baroque and Islamic styles, conceived in 1883 not for Lloyds but for the original business here, the Palsgrove Hotel. McLennan was a star at Royal Doulton; he was still in his toons when he arrived at the Lambeth Studios in 1877 and only a year later he won a silver medal at an Alexandra Palace exhibition.

It's no longer a bank, and at the time of writing the owners are looking for a new tenant. One hopes that it will at least be a restaurant again, so that these remarkable decorations can be seen in an appropriate context – preferably one serving flying fish.

# BATES' CAT

**73 JERMYN STREET ⊖ GREEN PARK**

**Opposite:** Binks in the original Jermyn Street shop, 2006
**Below:** Binks in Hilditch & Key, without his cigar, 2018

I suppose Jermyn Street may now be considered something of an anachronism, considering that it is an enclave for that rarest of shops – gentlemen's outfitters (and a cheese shop, still looking as if Eric Ravilious had just lithographed it). Here you will find proper shirts, ones that fit properly and leave enough material to tuck into one's trousers; shoes handmade in Northamptonshire; and every kind of hat, from bowlers to Henley boaters.

Bates was where you went for your Fischer Fedora or Ecuador Coffee Planter, and where, in 1921, a kitten strolled in and promptly took up residence. Binks was much loved by the staff and, after his demise in 1927, was honoured by a taxidermist and placed in a glass case wearing a top hat and smoking a cigar.

And there he remained, surrounded by beautifully-labelled hat boxes and with a notice exhorting a donation if you were only there to stare at him; until quite recently, when Bates suddenly disappeared. Now at Hilditch & Key, 73 Jermyn Street (more shirts), Binks is well and truly stuffed into a corner, *sans* cigar for the usual reasons involving the Tobacco Police.

# GREATER LONDON HOUSE

**HAMPSTEAD ROAD ⊖ MORNINGTON CRESCENT**

I first knew this stunning Art Deco building as the home of the advertising agency Young & Rubicam, creators of the slogan 'Beanz Meanz Heinz'. They weren't the first here though; this was once the Black Cat cigarette factory, properly known as Carreras, whose name has avoided the attentions of the Tobacco Police and has been preserved on the entablature. This building was originally the Arcadia Works, built here by Carreras in 1928. At the time it was both the world's largest cigarette factory and largest reinforced concrete building. Carreras were so proud of it that they put it on the back of their cigarette cards. The company adopted the cat as its symbol, doubtless influenced by the Egyptian cat-headed goddess Bastet discovered in Tutankhamen's tomb eight years earlier. With the rise of the Third Reich it was rumoured that Hitler fancied using the building as his UK headquarters, should his invasion plans succeed, just as he apparently earmarked the City of Oxford and the Grand Hotel in Scarborough as favoured places to dictate from.

The architects were ME and OH Collins, and AG Porri, but the Art Deco ornamentation was removed in the 1960s, the original bronze cats being sent out to Carreras factories in Basildon and Jamaica. Now it's all back, restored in 1999. Imperious Egyptian cats flank the doorways and Biblical reeds shoot up the columns. Best of all are the cats' heads in their recessed mounts – these black cats, as seen on the cigarette pack logo, are now fully equipped with wire whiskers to detect secret smokers.

# THE WESTMINSTER BRIDGE LION

**Opposite:** Keeping watch over Westminster Bridge
**Below:** Publicity material for the Lion Brewery

This white Coade stone lion stares imperiously out at Lambeth, an Aslan-like figure impervious to the crowds passing by his plinth. Coade stone isn't stone at all, but a ceramic substitute manufactured in Lambeth from 1769 until 1821, initially under the auspices of the firm's eponymous founder, Eleanor Coade. Its unique selling point was that delicate decoration could look as if it had been individually carved when it was actually mass produced, a great boon for the builders and architects of a rapidly-expanding London. So the lion is in fact an immense piece of pottery. We are often told that the 'recipe' for this magic substance was lost sometime after the manufacturing process was moved out of London to Stamford in Lincolnshire, but the British Museum has apparently successfully cracked the Coade Code.

This isn't the only deceptive thing about this magnificent beast. Sculpted by W.F. Woodington in 1837, he is the largest of three red-painted lions that once padded around the skyline of the Lion Brewery, which stood a little further downstream by the Charing Cross railway bridge. The brewery was blitzed in the war, and after the area was cleared in 1950 for the Festival of Britain, the site was occupied by the Royal Festival Hall. Mr. Woodington thoughtfully carved his initials and the exact date on one of the lion's paws: '24th May 1837', less than a month before Queen Victoria succeeded to the throne.

# LONDON SOULS

# HAWKSMOOR CHURCHES

**Previous spread:** Christ Church, Commercial Street, Spitalfields; built 1714-29
**Opposite page:** St.George-in-the-East, The Highway Stepney; built 1714-19
**Below:** St. Anne's, Newell Street, Limehouse; built 1714-30

You can never ignore a Hawksmoor church. Something about it will always draw you in, activate a 'hang-on-a-minute' moment. They look like churches and they appear to follow the brief as far as liturgical requirements go, but only just. They get lumped in with the baroque, but in my book they are simply Hawksmoor: among the most beautiful, enigmatic and slightly eerie churches in London. They are codes in white Portland stone still waiting to be deciphered. When the wooden scaffolding poles came off, the impact on early eighteenth-century sensibilities must have been like waking up to see Foster's Gherkin on the skyline.

Nicholas Hawksmoor (1661-1736) started his London career as a clerk to Sir Christopher Wren. He became his pupil, assistant and finally business partner, before working for John Vanbrugh. Both figures tended to overshadow his own achievements, leaving Hawksmoor as the 'back room boy'. But he was their friend, and they gave him the respect and encouragement that underpinned his own truly independent concepts. Hawksmoor designed many buildings, amongst them the Castle Howard Mausoleum and the west towers of Westminster Abbey. Here is his classic triumverate of East End churches, all built as a result of the New Churches Act of 1711.

# SIR RICHARD BURTON'S TOMB

**Opposite top:** St. Mary
Magdalen graveyard, Mortlake
**Opposite below left:** Tomb
detail (note the toy camel behind
the crucifix)
**Opposite below right:** Rear
ladder and window

Portraits of Sir Richard Francis Burton tend to show a rather cross-looking man with a big black crescent of a moustache and/ or impressive whiskers. His achievements were legion: apart from learning 25 languages and 40 dialects, he was one of the foremost Victorian explorers, travelling around and writing about Asia, Africa and South America. He also used his skills as a transalator to give us what is still recognised as the definitive text of *The Arabian Nights* – the publication of the first unexpurgated edition caused the usual fainting-fit of a Victorian scandal. His widow, Isabel Arundell, set light to his translation of *The Perfumed Garden*, but redeemed herself of book-burning by producing this startling and utterly original mausoleum for her husband on his death in 1890.

I found it on a dry, dusty summer day, the graveyard of St. Mary Magdalen in Mortlake having more of the atmosphere of an Italian *cimitero* than a South London burial ground. Surely a more appropriate monument to an explorer couldn't be made: a life-size stone tent complete with decorative fringing, moulded ropes and creases in the pretend canvas fabric. A crucifix is attached above where one assumes the entrance was, and on my visit, the cross was accompanied by a stuffed toy camel.

The biggest surprise is round the back of the tent, incongruously near to the back gardens of a Mortlake terrace. An iron ladder can be climbed up, leading to a window in the tent roof. When I got to the top, all I could see was my reflection and that of the still trees above, until I cupped my eyes to peer in through the glass. Immediately below, I could see a small altar and the remains of votive lights, and then, there they were – Richard and Isabel, either side of the tent, as if they were on some bizarre camping expedition with their coffins resting on foldaway beds. Disturbingly, Isabel's coffin lid was very slightly ajar. Everything was dusted in a patina of great age, and I left for a slow, thoughtful walk through the heat back to Mortlake station.

# THE TEMERAIRE CHAIRS

**ST. MARY THE VIRGIN, ROTHERHITHE ⊖ ROTHERHITHE**

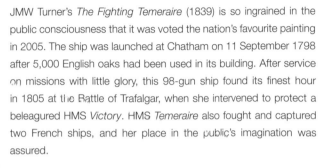

**Opposite:** The two Bishops' chairs on the north side of the church
**Below:** Underneath the paint and plaster on the supporting columns of the church are four ships' masts

JMW Turner's *The Fighting Temeraire* (1839) is so ingrained in the public consciousness that it was voted the nation's favourite painting in 2005. The ship was launched at Chatham on 11 September 1798 after 5,000 English oaks had been used in its building. After service on missions with little glory, this 98-gun ship found its finest hour in 1805 at the Battle of Trafalgar, when she intervened to protect a beleagured HMS *Victory*. HMS *Temeraire* also fought and captured two French ships, and her place in the public's imagination was assured.

One of her last services was as a prison ship, moored on the River Tamar until 1819, before she became a receiving ship, victualling depot and guard ship at Sheerness. In 1838, HMS *Temeraire* was towed (the subject of Turner's painting) from Sheerness to Beatson's yard in Rotherhithe, where she was broken up. One can easily imagine top-hatted timber merchants crawling like ants over the dismembered ship, their big wagons trundling fully-laden out of the yard. Much of this timber was utilised in house building, and oddly enough a great deal found itself turned into garden furniture. Here in St. Mary the Virgin, Rotherhithe, can be seen portions of the timber making two Bishops' chairs and an altar table, both bearing brass plaques telling of their illustrious heritage. Apparently, there were originally four such chairs, although the whereabouts of the other two remain unknown.

# WATCHER'S HUT, WANSTEAD

OVERTON DRIVE ⊖ WANSTEAD

**Opposite:** The churchyard and watcher's hut behind St. Mary's Church on Overton Drive in Wanstead

Wanstead can easily be missed as you arrive in London off the M11 and negotiate the Redbridge roundabout. To either side of Eastern Avenue are quiet suburban streets, in and around which are many reminders of 18th-century development that took advantage of the proximity of the popular coaching route to and from Colchester. To the south are Overton Drive and the church of St. Mary the Virgin, built 1787–90 by Thomas Hardwick in precisely-jointed ashlar. Walk round to the south side and a large leafy churchyard opens up, filled with interesting tombs under the trees. And, hidden amongst the shrubberies, is this curious tapering stone sentry box, built in memory of the Wilton family in 1831.

This is a watcher's hut, where a sentry would have guarded the churchyard. This was a time of body snatchers, when fresh corpses for medical research were hard to come by unless removed from their graves at the earliest opportunity, under the cover of darkness. Corpses were invaluable for dissection in anatomy lectures, and those responsible for these unholy thefts quickly became known as 'resurrectionists'. The only legal supply of bodies at this time were the remains of those sent to the gallows by a court. A watchman was paid to sit in the sentry box and look out for the light of a swaying lantern, and to listen for the first sharp incision of a spade into mouldering soil.

The year after the arrival of this shelter, the Anatomy Act of 1832 was passed, which brought the unsavoury and ghoulish practice to an end. But what an elegant solution this is, for what is after all just an open-sided hut. Imagine what we would have to put up with here today if an invasion of body snatchers became popular again. I suppose the best a night watchman could hope for would be something pressed out of durable plastic, looking rather like a Portaloo.

29

# GATE PILLARS, DEPTFORD

**DEPTFORD GREEN ⇌ DEPTFORD**

**Opposite:** A grisly welcome to St. Nicholas church in a Deptford back street

The original church of St. Nicholas was demolished and rebuilt in 1697, but it still retains the medieval tower. In the churchyard is a rare eighteenth-century example of a charnel house, a repository for old bones disturbed during interments, and inside the church are carvings, attributed to Grinling Gibbons, of Ezekiel's Vision of The Valley of Dry Bones. Gibbons is also thought to have been responsible for the pair of gruesome death's-heads on the churchyard entrance pillars.

And that was going to be all I could say about these particularly startling sculptures, until one day I was looking at Hogarth's painting *Chairing the Member,* and there in the background of a riotous mid-eighteenth century election scene is one of these pillars, or at least one very much like it. A chimney sweep is cheekily placing a pair of spectacles on the nose of the skull.

# HIGHGATE CEMETERY

SWAIN'S LANE, HIGHGATE ⊖ ARCHWAY

Many will know of the curious and sombre delights of this cemetery from John Gay's stunning black and white photographs in his aptly named book, *Highgate Cemetery: Victorian Valhalla*, which focused on the cemetery's western side. This wilderness of graves, vaults and monuments has slowly emerged from the stranglehold of vociferous plants, with angels peering down in benefaction through the leaves, faithful dogs sleeping and crying children clutching rustic crosses.

From Kentish Town, Camden, Belsize Park and St. John's Wood they came. Bankers, bank clerks, doctors, poets, grocers, grocers' boys. All equal now, making their final journeys up from the pigeon-haunted towers and steeples of the metropolis, engraved glass hearses pulled by black-plumed horses that nodded and snorted up through the dark shades of Swain's Lane to this steep hillside, to join Faraday, Galsworthy, the Rossettis and, in 1853, John Atcheler, horse slaughterer to Queen Victoria.

The paths twist and turn upwards from the buttressed turrets of the cemetery chapels, past countless leaning crosses and draped urns, until an extraordinary sight starts to appear through the trees. A tunnel entrance, cut into the hillside, is flanked by pairs of bulbous Egyptian columns. Once inside, the gloom slowly dissipates to reveal rows of vault doorways on each side. The ground rises up to the light, where a ring of sunken tombs, each with a classical or Pharoahic entrance doorway, are guarded over by the black, silhouetted branches of a spreading cedar.

The Egyptian Avenue and Circle of Lebanon are the eerie showpieces on these 37 acres of Highgate Hill, established by the London Cemetery Company in 1836. The Friends of Highgate Cemetery have worked miracles in restoring so much for us to see, and a guided tour is a must if you want to know the stories that go with these memorials from the past.

# ST. PANCRAS GARDENS

PANCRAS ROAD 🚇 KING'S CROSS ST. PANCRAS

**Opposite:** The Soane family vault, complete with a Soanian dome surmounting the pillars
**Below:** A K6 Soanian-domed telephone box
**Below right:** The highly-Victorianised Norman church of St. Pancras

St. Pancras Gardens sit just to the north-west of St. Pancras International railway station. Originally this was the churchyard of St. Pancras Old Church, which lays claim to being one of the earliest Christian sites in the country. These days it's more of a park for Camden dog walkers, but although the tombs are now somewhat sparse, there is one that still has an echo through to our times. Architect Sir John Soane designed a vault for his wife in 1815, which, before his own interment in 1837, also became the grave of his eldest son. The roof is a classic Soanian dome, which in the 1920s became a great influence on Sir Giles Gilbert Scott's new red telephone boxes, one of the finest pieces of industrial design.

In 1866, the Midland Railway needed to appropriate a section of the churchyard for their lines into St. Pancras station, and another architect, Arthur Blomfield, deputed one of his staff to superintend the respectful removal of many hundreds of coffins and bones. This was Thomas Hardy, who later wrote of the experience in his poem *The Levelled Churchyard*: 'We late-lamented, resting here, / Are mixed to human jam'. Indeed both Hardy and Blomfield witnessed a coffin breaking open to reveal one skeleton and two skulls.

EACH PLAQUE COMMEMORATES AN ACT OF BRAVERY – NOT GREAT DEEDS IN BATTLE, BUT SIMPLE ACTS OF EXTREME HEROISM AND SELF-SACRIFICE.

MARY·ROGERS
STEWARDESS OF THE STEL
MAR·30·1899
SELF SACRIFICED BY GIVING
HER LIFE BELT AND VOLUNTARI
GOING DOWN IN THE
SINKING SHIP

ARTHUR STRANGE
CARMAN OF LONDON·AND
MARK TOMLINSON
ON A·DESPERATE VENTURE
TO SAVE TWO GIRLS FROM A
QUICKSAND IN LINCOLNSHIRE·
WERE THEMSELVES ENGULFED·
AUG·25·1902·

# POSTMAN'S PARK

KING EDWARD STREET ⊖ ST. PAUL'S

**Opposite above left:** The memorial loggia in Postman's Park
**Opposite below:** Memorial plaques by William De Morgan (right) and Doulton (left)

This little oasis of green between King Edward Street and Aldersgate Street was once the churchyard of St. Botolph's, Aldersgate. At one time opposite the Royal Mail offices, this was a peaceful haven for postmen having their lunches. All along an eastward-facing wall are beautifully-lettered ceramic plaques, protected from inclement weather by a lean-to loggia. Each plaque commemorates an act of bravery – not great deeds in battle, but simple acts of extreme heroism and self-sacrifice in often violent circumstances, involving catastrophes like runaway trains and sinking ships. These are commendations of ordinary people in extraordinary situations, like William Drake, who, in 1869, averted serious injury to a lady whose horses 'became unmanageable through the breaking of the carriage pole.' The lady is anonymous; it is William's name that has survived. As has that of David Selves, who 'supported his drowning playfellow and sank with him clasped in his arms'; Amelia Kennedy, who died in a burning house in Stoke Newington trying to save her sister; and Thomas Griffin, who died searching for his mate after an explosion in a Battersea sugar refinery.

The plaques were the inspiration of the Victorian artist George Frederic Watts (he sculpted *Physical Energy* for Kensington Gardens) who was particularly moved by the story of Alice Ayres, a live-in maid who successfully rescued her employer's children from a burning house and then died as she attempted to save herself by jumping from a window. He quite rightly thought that these acts of selfless bravery should be commemorated, but the idea didn't continue for long after Watts' death in 1904. William De Morgan designed and produced the simple but effective lettering and decorations on the original plaques. After Watts' death, his wife continued the project, but after De Morgan decided he was going to be a novelist, she asked Doulton's of Lambeth to produce these plaques. Mary Watts was not so happy with the result and decided to concentrate her efforts on the Watts Memorial Chapel in Compton, Surrey. The idea

3

**Above:** Memorial plaques by William De Morgan

EART DRIVER

EAN FIREMAN

SOR·EXPRESS

8·1898

CALDED & BURNT

HEIR LIVES IN

THE TRAIN

STE

SELF

HER

has now been resurrected, and the latest plaque pays tribute to Leigh Pitt, who on 7 June 2007 rescued a nine-year-old boy from a Thamesmead canal, but drowned in his attempt to haul himself over the high canal walls.

# LONDON TRADE

COUPE des VOITURETTES 1907    NAUDIN sur SIZAIRE et NAUDIN

GRAND PRIX Dieppe de l'A.C.F. 1908    LAUTENSCHLAGER sur MERCÉDÈS

# THE MICHELIN BUILDING

FULHAM ROAD ⊖ SOUTH KENSINGTON

**Previous spread:** Canteen of the Hoover building. See page 50
**Opposite centre left and bottom right:** Detail in Lucan Place; Michelin racing successes in 1907 and 1908 in tiles
**Opposite centre right:** An early manifestation of Bibendum, Michelin's trademark made from tyres
**Following spread:** Michelin Building from Fulham Road

The wonderfully ebullient exterior of the Michelin Building hid a functionality that was perfectly in sync with the burgeoning motor age. Opened in 1911, this was the UK headquarters for Michelin, the French company from Clermont-Ferrand that led the world with pneumatic tyres. The front entrance, where until quite recently you could buy lobsters and flowers from suitably Gallic Citroën *camionettes*, was the tyre-fitting bay and, as your car was put onto a 6-ton weighbridge, you could wait for new tyres by passing the time in the Touring Office, consulting maps and guides.

The designer of this *tour de force* in Brompton Cross was François Espinasse. We know virtually nothing about him, other than that he worked for Michelin, and the only other building he appears to have designed was the company's more subdued head office in Paris. He made the London building a brightly coloured three-dimensional advertisement, his starting point the cigar-chomping Bibendum, the Michelin man made from tyres. Much of this was achieved by the use of 'Marmo' facing tiles, something of an experiment for the manufacturers, Burmantofts.

But perhaps the most awe-inspiring parts of this building are the 34 tiled panels that race down Sloane Avenue and Lucan Place. Here the successes of Michelin tyres in cycle and motor races are celebrated, with ceramic tiles designed by Ernest Montaut and manufactured by Gilardoni Fils et Cie. They continue around the entrance hall inside. For the superb restoration of this remarkable building we must be grateful for the collaboration in the mid-1980s of Paul Hamlyn and Terence Conran, whose emporium still occupies the site on Brompton Cross.

# BERRY BROS. & RUDD

**Opposite:** One of the window shutters in Pickering Place
**Below:** The alley leading to Pickering Place

It's very easy to walk past Pickering Place without noticing it's there. I only spotted it because a chap came out onto St. James's Street like someone striding out of a brick wall in a Harry Potter film. It is very narrow, opening into London's smallest square, where the last duel in England was fought.

But that's not the Peculiar. Going back down the alley, I noticed that the walls were lined with glossily-painted wooden panels. Closer inspection revealed that some of them had dissected parts of lettering on them in signwriters' gilt: the same style that graces the frontage of Berry Bros. & Rudd, next door at No. 3 St. James's Street. I assumed that they were doors to some additional storage space.

Berry Bros. can trace its history back to 1698, making it undisputedly one of the oldest wine merchants in the world, although the sign tells of a previous business as a grocer selling teas and coffees. The cellars spread out underground as far as Pall Mall; at 8,000 square feet, they are the largest working cellars in London. That's space for 10,000 bottles. But this is no off-licence; you don't come in here and ask for a bottle of Blue Nun, as evidenced by the sloping wooden floors, oak panelled walls and a curious sit-on weighing machine that has endured the likes of Byron, Evelyn Waugh, Churchill and a naked Beau Brummell (he insisted on this *déshabillé* so that the measuring would be accurate).

On the pretext of checking the case rate on some obscure Burgundy, I asked about the wooden-lined alley next door. 'They are our window shutters, sir.' What a wonderful thing: heavy boards daubed in countless coats of dark green paint, slid in order into grooves running down the alley. Sadly, they're not used on the windows now, but they are still a Peculiar worth searching for. And do seek out the shop; although now mainly based at 63 Pall Mall on the corner, the original is still there to be seen at 3 St. James's Street.

# HOOVER BUILDING

**WESTERN AVENUE, PERIVALE ⊖ PERIVALE**

**Right:** Advertisement for a Hoover
Model 50 Cylinder Cleaner
**Below:** Main factory frontage

This is '30s Art Deco architecture at its finest. Designed in 1931-5 by Wallis, Gilbert & Partners, Nikolaus Pevsner said it was 'Perhaps the most offensive of the modernistic atrocities along this road of typical bypass factories' 20 years after it was built. Few would agree with this condemnation now, particularly as the similar and nearby Firestone tyre factory, by the same architects, was illegally bulldozed in 1980.

If the sun's out, I can't go by it on the A40 out of London without stopping and photographing it again, thinking of all those sleek saloons careening out to Chiltern country houses in the '30s, the driver perhaps giving it a cursory glance but his passenger thinking 'Actually, we need a Hoover vacuum cleaner'. What looks like an aerodrome terminal (page 42) is in fact the canteen, designed by J.W. MacGregor in 1938, and behind the main Hoover Building frontage is now a cleverly-positioned Tesco superstore. Every little helps.

# SPITALFIELDS MARKET

**CRISPIN STREET ⊖ LIVERPOOL STREET**

**Opposite:** Donovan Bros' first shop in Crispin Street, Spitalfields Market, photographed in the late 1980s but still there in a less characterful guise

Donovan Brothers are now in Orpington, Kent. They presumably left not long after I photographed one of their first shops in Crispin Street, very early one morning in the '80s.

As I snapped away at the Spitalfields traders loading up vans with fruit and veg (one of them very obligingly putting an apple crate over his head for me) I then found this essential part of the business, painted a dusky red and gloriously scruffy like everything else. The market has gone now, replaced by City boys and girls washed up from Bishopsgate, drinking skinny lattes and staring at pictures of fruit on their mobiles. This frontage got painted a more hushed green and cream as the street lost its patina of lettuce leaves and squashed apples, but thankfully the hand-painted characterful lettering still survives as a reminder that paper bags really are a supremely recyclable product.

# SMITHFIELD MARKET

 FARRINGDON

**Opposite:** One of the four domed towers that sit at the corners of the original building, erected in 1866-7 by Sir Horace Jones
**Below left:** The last of the tripe dressers in Lindsey Street, now demolished
**Below right:** The current un-butcher-like colour scheme

Smithfield is London's wholesale meat market, a nocturnal city of carcasses where tradesmen eat steaks in pubs at six in the morning. By midday, most of the serious business of humping meat about is over, the loud hums of refrigerated vehicles and shouts from white-hatted butchers subdued until the next day; but at any time here there is always the echo of Hogarth and Dickens. It's not difficult to imagine the distant past: tightly packed cattle being driven into pens made from wooden hurdles, the flies, the heat, the gutteral shouts and red kites wheeling over it all. Every now and then, the market was cleared away so that they could burn somebody at the stake, *Stakes and Steaks: A History of Smithfield Market.*

Glass-eyed developers are now turning their attention towards Smithfield's hinterland, and one does worry about all this carnivorous activity being banished out to the fringes. Let's hope it stays: the only wholesale market now left in the City.

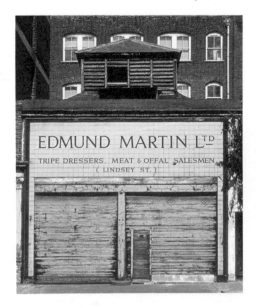

EDMUND MARTIN L^TD
TRIPE DRESSERS. MEAT & OFFAL SALESMEN
( LINDSEY ST.)

# BRITISH EMPIRE EXHIBITION

**Opposite:** Palace of Arts
**Below:** Palace of Industry
**Bottom:** Frederick Herrick's
exhibition symbol

In 1924, the British Empire Exhibition spread over 216 acres in Wembley. The far-flung colonial outposts gathered together in the mother country: New Zealand showing off their dairy farms, Australia demonstrating how much cotton it grew, India waving the flag with elephants and pictures of the Taj Mahal and Canada amazing the world with a model of The Prince of Wales made out of butter. The whole enterprise was opened by King George V on radio, after which The King and Queen sat bolt upright on a miniature railway as it hurtled amongst the pavilions and amusements. There were the usual exhibition novelties: a kiosk made up of a ziggurat of Sharp's Toffee tins topped off with a parrot, and a giant globe crowned with an Oxo cube. But the biggest impact came with the purpose-built pavilions – Palaces of Industry, Arts and Engineering. Towering over them all was the Empire Stadium, opened the year before to accommodate the 1923 FA Cup final. The goal of these monuments was to 'evoke the permanence of the imperial glories of antiquity', and the palaces, with their windowless reinforced concrete walls, certainly had a whiff of the Egyptian tomb about them.

Permanent no more. The twin-towered stadium, beloved by generations of football fans, has gone, replaced by a building that is not nearly as original. Everything else except Wembley Park Station has also been destroyed, including these two battered survivors: the Palace of Industry and the much smaller Palace of Arts. I'm so glad I photographed them back in 2006, because now, although I knew I was in the right place, all I could see were the usual indifferent blocks of new flats. Everything to do with the British Empire Exhibition of 1924 has now vanished, except for four lions' heads. Three reside in a council depot, while one sits up on a plinth, as if to remind us of just how fabulous all this was. The estate is now called Wembley City, and looks like the setting for a dystopian novel.

# LIBERTY

GREAT MARLBOROUGH STREET ⊖ OXFORD CIRCUS
THE LEE, BUCKS. ⇄ GREAT MISSENDEN

**Below left:** Liberty store in Great Marlborough Street
**Below right:** The Admiral Howe figurehead from HMS *Impregnable*, now at The Lee in Buckinghamshire

It is perhaps well-known that the Liberty store just off Regent Street was built in 1922-24, utilising the timbers from two Royal Navy warships: HMS *Impregnable* and HMS *Hindustan.* The former was the last wooden warship built, commissioned in the 1860s and formerly called HMS *Howe* after Admiral of the Fleet, Lord Howe (1726-99). The figurehead was taken to The Lee in Buckinghamshire and erected outside the back entrance to the Manor, home of Captain Ivor Stewart-Liberty. On his death in 1952, it was moved to Pipers, where it could be seen at the gate, until more recently when it was housed in a wooden shed.

My father told me that not long after its original positioning by the road, he rode his bicycle up from Great Missenden station and ended up in the ditch in fright, having seen this be-wigged head staring at him. His acetylene bike lamp went out and refused to re-light, and he continued his way in the dark to Lee Common, doubtless wondering what he had actually witnessed.

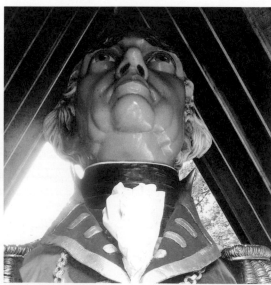

# TWININGS

Twinings' flagship shop, still at the Golden Lyon

Opposite the Law Courts on the Strand is the original Twinings shop, where you can still buy fine teas (including the evocatively named 'English Breakfast', so redolent of a crisply folded newspaper and the aroma of pipe tobacco) and fruit and herb infusions. The two Chinese men and the lion are made from that ubiquitous material, Coade stone (see the South Bank Lion on Westminster Bridge, pages 18-19), and have lounged above the shop door since 1787. The lion, commissioned by Richard Twining, the founder's grandson, reminds us of the original Twinings store: The Golden Lyon of 1707. Richard Twining had persuaded William Pitt to reduce the Surrender Tax on tea, which at this time was exclusively imported from China, hence the arrival of these beautifully-painted figures.

Twinings has the oldest commercial logo still in use. Here in the flagship store you can sample flavours at the Loose Tea Bar, experience a masterclass with a Tea Ambassador, or make sure you're well stocked-up with Earl Grey, Lady Grey, or a Salted Caramel infusion.

# LONDON MOVES

# TEMPLE BAR

PATERNOSTER SQUARE 🚇 ST. PAUL'S

The Temple Bar marked the boundary between the Cities of London and Westminster. It was a Portland stone gateway straddling the point where Fleet Street becomes the Strand, at the spot marked today by a fearsome dragon, rearing up to blast his fiery breath at Westminster.

Sir Christopher Wren is the most likely designer of this dramatic piece of Baroque architecture, with its niches, statues and overflowing cornucopias surrounding the central arch and the two dark and narrow pedestrian tunnels. Completed in 1672, it quickly became a focal point for ceremonies and processions, and, this being the seventeenth century, was often embellished with the severed heads of traitors.

As London's vehicular traffic increased, the Temple Bar became a noisy bottleneck and, once the north side of the street was demolished to make way for the new Royal Courts of Justice, its future was in jeopardy. It survived *in situ* until 1878, when the component parts were removed and stored in a yard off Farringdon Street.

Ten years later, brewer Sir Henry Meux purchased it wholesale and re-erected it as an eyecatcher at Theobalds, his estate near Cheshunt in Hertfordshire. His wife hid a time capsule amongst the stones.

That would have been the end of story, except that in 2004 it was dismantled again and moved back to the City, where it was reassembled in the new Paternoster Square next to St. Paul's. Almost back home. And yes, they found the time capsule. Most of it was a fine mulch of nineteenth-century paper, but there were some coins and a piece of the *Sporting Times* dated 7 January 1888 with the clearly discernible word 'Wizard'. Exactly the right word for a building that has magically appeared in three different locations in its lifetime.

# MIDLAND RAILWAY WATER POINT

**YORK WAY ⊖ KING'S CROSS ST.PANCRAS**

**Opposite:** View from the Regent's Park Canal

Sliding along the icy towpath of the Regent's Park Canal, past the boarded-up Fish and Coal Depot next to St.Pancras International, I discovered this magnificent survivor from the Age of Steam. Built in 1867 for the Midland Railway, it echoes Giles Gilbert Scott's station frontage in so many ways. His design for the Gothic blind-arcaded tower is in the same red Nottingham brick with Ancaster stone detailing, supporting an iron tank encased in pillared masonry. The big chimney tells of the massive stove they must have got going in winter months to stop the water freezing. Towers like this were obviously essential in the days of steam locomotives, particularly at a big terminus like St.Pancras that not only had busy arrivals and departures at the passenger platforms, but also continual workings in the goods yards.

With the arrival of the new continental lines into St.Pancras International, the existence of this water point came under threat, but it survived by being moved 700 yards from its original location. There is so much to appreciate here; these evocative remains are evidence that the Victorian era was like an enormous shout, still sending its echoes down to us from the nineteenth century.

# PRINCE ALBERT'S MODEL DWELLING HOUSE

**KENNINGTON PARK ⊖ OVAL**

Queen Victoria's consort, Prince Albert, was a prime mover in the whole staggering enterprise that was the Great Exhibition of 1851. But there is a much humbler building that he initiated that now stands forgotten in a South London park.

His 'Model Dwelling House' was one of the 1851 exhibits that could stand inclement weather, and so, along with traction engines and awe-inspiring lumps of Welsh coal, it was exhibited outside the glass arena. It was designed around the Prince's ideas for workers' housing, by Henry Roberts, the architect for the very worthy-sounding 'Society for Improving the Condition of the Labouring Classes'. The premise was simple: a group of four flats sharing a communal open-well staircase that became a feature of thousands of mid-Victorian dwellings. It didn't help the poor, however. Flats like these were only affordable for comparatively well-paid artisans, a common dilemma for workers' housing in the nineteenth century.

The Prince's model dwellings were taken down and moved here to Kennington in an equally sylvan setting.

# WELLINGTON &
# THE CONSTITUTION ARCH

⊖ HYDE PARK CORNER ⇌ ALDERSHOT

**Below left:** The *Victory Quadriga* on the Constitution Arch
**Below right:** The original statue, removed to Aldershot in Hampshire

The Constitution Arch sits marooned on a traffic island, and whilst not quite an Arc de Triomphe, it is at least a hub of roads and traffic with the same whirling, noisy spirit. The Arch once stood behind Decimus Burton's Hyde Park Corner Screen, trumpeting the exit from the park towards Buckingham Palace. Burton also designed the Arch, but couldn't believe his eyes when he saw the sheer scale of the equestrian statue of Wellington that was placed on top. He objected to it in the strongest terms, even leaving money in his will to have it taken away. Finally, the Arch was moved to its present site in 1883 and Wellington was taken off his plinth. In 1911, Adrian Jones' more appropriately-scaled *Victory Quadriga* was lowered into position.

Matthew Cotes Wyatt's immense statue was led out to the Hampshire woods and erected on a bluff of land above All Saints Garrison Church in Aldershot. Wellington on his charger, Copenhagen, rises above the surrounding landscape like some mythical warrior giant arriving at a critical moment of battle.

LIKE SO MUCH IN LONDON,
THESE CURIOSITIES
HAVE TRAVELLED THE
METROPOLIS LIKE LOST
SOULS, IN THIS CASE
SINCE THE SIXTEENTH
CENTURY WHEN THEY
ORIGINALLY ADORNED A
NEW REPLACEMENT FOR
THE LUD GATE, ONE OF THE
ENTRANCES TO THE CITY.

# LUD GATE SURVIVORS

**FLEET STREET, PILGRIM STREET ⊖ TEMPLE, BLACKFRIARS**

**Opposite top:** Lud and Sons
**Opposite centre:** Queen Elizabeth I
**Opposite bottom:** Corner stone,
Pilgrim Street

One darkening winter's afternoon I stepped off Fleet Street into the yard of St. Dunstan-in-the-West church in order to get a closer look at the lettering on the magazine offices next door. Curious about something in the gloomy entrance to the church vestry, I discovered these sepulchral figures (opposite) backed-up against the wall as if engaged in some macabre game of hide-and-seek.

Like so much in London, these curiosities have travelled the metropolis like lost souls, in this case since the sixteenth century when they originally adorned a new replacement for the Lud Gate, one of the entrances to the City. They are in fact depictions of King Lud and his sons, and once stared out down towards the Fleet River at what is now Ludgate Circus. Every reference I have come across concerning King Lud, with or without his offspring, is very vague as to his origins. Some think he gave his name to London itself; many agree that he could have been a king ruling around the time of the Roman invasion; others think he was just a made-up kingly figure used for political purposes. Man or myth, he will always be associated with London's more shadowy histories. Lud Gate was sold for £148 in 1760 and, like the other city gates, pulled down. The statues, including the one of Elizabeth I seen here in her niche, were rescued by the Marquis of Hertford, who used them as garden ornaments at his Regent's Park villa. The next century saw them brought to Fleet Street when St. Dunstan's was rebuilt in 1829-33.

Some time later, I nearly tripped over a stone embedded in a corner of Pilgrim Street, just off Ludgate, only to discover that this too was a survivor of the old gate. I imagine it was recycled to protect the building from vehicle wheels in the narrow confines of the lane.

# ALL HALLOWS CHURCH TOWER

**CHERTSEY ROAD ⇌ TWICKENHAM**

All Hallows tower from Erncroft Way, Twickenham

An incongruous seventeenth-century City church tower by Sir Christopher Wren can be spotted in the suburbs at Twickenham. The church of All Hallows originally resided in Lombard Street, before becoming unsafe and being pulled down in 1938. The white Portland stone tower was moved out to Chertsey Road, a landmark to look out for whilst coursing the string of roundabouts on the A316.

# BATTISHILL STREET GARDENS

**NAPIER TERRACE, ISLINGTON ⊖ HIGHBURY & ISLINGTON**

Details of Musgrave Watson's sculpture, designed for a building in Threadneedle Street

Walk down into the little sunken garden in Napier Terrace and one is confronted by this extraordinary sight. Around two sides of the first part of the garden is a relief sculpture with flouncing Mercurys and naked men astride horses, another piece of London far from its original site. It's as if buildings explode and send all their constituent parts into some crazy orbit, until they're magnetically drawn to an alternative resting place.

This work of art was chipped out in 1842 by Musgrave Watson for the House of Commerce in Threadneedle Street, and removed to University College when the building was demolished in 1922. A piece of early Victorian art designed to impress the hell out of stove pipe-hatted financiers, this piece has been brought down to earth in an Islington park for everyone to enjoy.

The new setting is perfect; the relief forms a magical backdrop to well-tended plants and a tiny pond, which reflects the detail darkly amongst the floating leaves.

# QUEEN ANNE'S ALCOVE

**KENSINGTON GARDENS ⊖ LANCASTER GATE**

A very superior summer house, the ultimate gazebo, designed by Sir Christopher Wren

This is an architectural rarity – a triumphal garden building by Wren. Like so many of London's curiosities, Queen Anne's Alcove has moved, travelling from the opposite side of the park to its current position, where it turns its back on the Bayswater Road by the Marlborough Gate. It had become a haunt of 'undesirable personages' at its original site. Certainly, there was enough room for them.

This oversized summer house was built in 1705, and, with its towering Corinthian columns and an awe-inspiring curve of wood panelling as a back rest to the seat, it almost seems out-of-scale here in the park. Perhaps it would have been more at home at the end of a three-mile avenue on a Norfolk estate, flanked by dark Scots firs.

# LONDON BRIDGE ALCOVE

**GUY'S HOSPITAL, ST. THOMAS STREET ⊖ LONDON BRIDGE**

A quieter and more secluded life for a former London Bridge alcove

The first stone London Bridge opened in 1209, with rows of houses ranging across 19 arches. Amazingly, these buildings survived until the mid-eighteenth century, when Robert Taylor and George Dance removed them and placed stone alcoves, complete with seats, on top of each pier of the original bridge. One imagines them to have been quickly and gratefully utilised by footpads and prostitutes. When finally the inevitable road-widening occurred in the early twentieth century, the alcoves were removed, but three survived, one to rest here for the use of doctors and nurses at Guy's Hospital, and two that were carted out to Victoria Park in Hackney. They are constructed with Portland stone, and this alcove was bought by Guy's Hospital for ten guineas and re-erected here in 1861.

# CRYSTAL PALACE PARK, SYDENHAM

Contemporary postcard of Crystal Palace

Sometimes, when we lose a building, its ground plan is quickly built on and the spirit of its presence erased. The ghosts of others hang around for much longer, especially if the space is unfilled. Here, overlooking south London, was one of the largest and most impressive structures ever built.

After its removal from Hyde Park a few weeks after the closure of the Great Exhibition of 1851, the Crystal Palace was brought here to be re-erected and enlarged by half again. Two tall Italianate water towers were built by Brunel at either end, and a series of terraces and steps led down to a vast park with ornamental lakes. Eighty-nine fire engines from all over London failed to stop the Crystal Palace from transforming itself into a twisted glassless frame on 30 November, 1936: the night of the apocalyptic fire that could be seen as far away as Brighton. Brunel's water towers survived, but were taken down during the Second World War to prevent their use as navigational aids by enemy bombers.

6104

Crystal Palace.

# CRYSTAL PALACE, HYDE PARK SURVIVORS

⊖ SOUTH KENSINGTON ⇌ PETERBOROUGH

**Below left:** The Coalbrookdale Gates, swung open by a Beefeater in 1851 for Queen Victoria
**Below right:** The Holme Fen Post near Yaxley, Peterborough, Cambridgeshire

...However, there are at least two reminders of the Great Exhibition of 1851 that never made the journey into South London. The original Coalbrookdale cast-iron entrance gates from inside the exhibition are now at the west end of the South Carriage Drive in Hyde Park. And out on a Cambridgeshire fen is probably the most curious reminder of this extraordinary glass palace.

The Great Exhibition coincided with the draining by John Lawrence of one of the last great tracts of original fenland, Whittlesey Mere. He picked up a cast-iron column from Hyde Park during the great dismantling (one does wonder how this happened) and drove it down through 22 feet of undrained peat to the underlying clay on Holme Fen near Peterborough. The idea was to measure how much peat shrinkage would occur, and by 1955 the column was twelve feet above ground. Today so much of it has been revealed the post now needs a set of iron supports to stop it toppling over, and is joined by other posts also pressed into service, all in an enclosure surrounded by silver birch trees.

# MATHERS:
# WHALE OIL
## EXTRACTION

GOODLUC

# LONDON LETTERS

# HEATH ROAD, TWICKENHAM

**Opposite and previous spread:** A brief moment in the sun for a painted wall sign after a poster hoarding was removed
**Below:** A 1950s Armstrong Siddeley

It's a little unfair to include this great rarity, because it was very quickly painted over and probably obliterated forever.

Like many London ghost signs though, could it suddenly reappear, as it did for me? These automobile names from the distant past (with the obvious exception of Vauxhall) had a few brief moments in the sun when a poster hoarding was taken down on the corner of Tennyson Avenue. This remarkable sign must have been painted before the Second World War.

Surviving virtually intact under all those exhortations to buy baked beans and washing powder, the clue to the date comes from 'Terraplane', a product of the American Hudson Motor Company, which last produced a car under this stand-alone name in 1937. The other names are a roll-call of now vanished stalwarts of the British motor industry: Standard, Riley, Singer and the posh Armstrong Siddeley.

79

# FOX & ANCHOR

**CHARTERHOUSE STREET ⊖ FARRINGDON**

Sunlight and shadow in the Fox & Anchor porch

The Fox & Anchor is a classic late Victorian pub with mahogany doors, etched glass and the ghosts of market porters who once swung in from Smithfield Market. A little bit posher now, with 'boutique bedrooms', on this day the porch was as remarkable for the tricks that low winter sunshine plays as it seeks its way to highlight forgotten corners, as it was for the beautiful Art Nouveau tiling. Probably made by Doulton's down in Lambeth, the richness of colour and design still appears as fresh as the day the pub furnishers carefully fitted the tiles into place.

# DOG & DUCK

**BATEMAN STREET ⊖ TOTTENHAM COURT ROAD**

A superbly florid exhortation to drink seltzer at the Dog & Duck

In a classic narrow Soho pub, this mirror dominates the wall opposite the bar. There was once a vogue for reproducing pub mirrors, but they could never compare to this glorious original for Struve's Brighton Seltzer. John Constable and Dante Gabriel Rossetti drank at this bar, but since the present building was only built in 1897, we should really perhaps mention author George Orwell and *chanteuse* Madonna.

# HOPE (SUFFERANCE) WHARF

**ST. MARYCHURCH STREET ⊖ ROTHERHITHE**

A building still proudly bearing the evidence of its maritime origins

I have always been intrigued by this lettering on a wall in St. Marychurch Street in Rotherhithe. The sign not only reminds us of the existence of Hope Wharf, but also of the curious adjunct 'sufferance' that once appeared in many wharf names along the Thames. During the eighteenth century, shipping traffic had grown to such an extent that the 'legal' wharves sanctioned to ship and unload cargo were totally inadequate for the amount of trade. So other wharves, particularly on the south bank, took in business under what was known as 'a sufferance' – that is, 'by tacit consent but without express permission'.

So much of London's docklands has metamorphosed into riverside residences, and much has disappeared. But in this small corner of Rotherhithe one can still faintly detect what it must have been like – minus the creaking of cranes and shouts of stevedores, of course.

# ORCHARD PLACE

⊖ EAST INDIA

*Mather's lettering clings on amongst more recent additions*

A 1595 map shows that there really was an orchard here at one time, belonging to John Churchman, a merchant tailor. Not many apples and pears now, as the last remnants of dockland buildings and their attendant ephemera are slowly eroded. Orchard Place leads down to Trinity Buoy Wharf, and on the right you will see this extraordinary wall still shouting the detail of a long-extinct industry. Mather's started the noxious work of boiling and processing whale blubber here in 1784, in what was the most inaccessible part of Poplar.

This peninsula, formed by the River Lea as it meanders into the Thames, was known since the fourteenth century as Goodluck Hope. The name has been appropriated for a new development that fortunately shows that, although London is constantly evolving, sensitive architecture echoing the heritage of the area is still welcomed.

# QUALITY CHOP HOUSE
**FARRINGDON ROAD ⊖ FARRINGDON**

Reassuring words for past working-class customers at the Quality Chop House

The Quality Chop House has been on the Farringdon Road since the 1870s. There have been several manifestations, but I can say from gastronomic experience that it's probably now at its best. Working with just a handful of small farms, the Quality Chop House promises you will always be able to get to grips with a chop and sit bolt upright on the collegiate-style seating (although at busy times you might have to share with other *bon viveurs*).

As I did the tucking-in, my fellow diner nodded at me and pointed at the top of the windows with a fork. The lettering talks of the time when this was a real café and served prodigious helpings of porridge, kippers and bubble 'n' squeak, most likely only to working-class blokes. Another sign reads 'London's Noted Cup Of Tea'. To help you, I have of course reversed the photograph (it also makes it look better with the picture opposite).

# LAMB & FLAG, COVENT GARDEN

'Dining' yes, 'Club Room' no, '1st Floor' yes

The Lamb & Flag is on Rose Street, and is often so full that customers spill out on summer evenings. At the side of the pub is a narrow passageway where, in 1679, the poet John Dryden was done over by a gang of thugs on behalf of the dissolute John Wilmot, the 2nd Earl of Rochester. Wilmot also wrote a considerable amount of poetry, including telling the newly restored Charles II: ' *...London is Itself the nation, not metropolis...*' Upstairs is now called the Dryden Room.

Fighting became the norm at the pub itself (formerly known as The Coopers Arms until 1833). In the early nineteenth century, it gained the nickname 'The Bucket of Blood' due to the frequent bare-knuckle fights that took place there. I have always been intrigued by this sign, which you only see when you're going down the stairs on the way out. This theatrical illuminated box was made by J.H.Golding of Stoke Newington, and just before handing this book over to the publisher I rang the pub to ask about it and a girl said "What sign?"

# SEVEN STARS

**CAREY STREET**  **HOLBORN**

**Opposite:** Seven Stars Doors Inside
**Below:** The double doors at the Seven Stars

The Private Counter door signs are an indication of what to expect in this very traditional and eccentric pub at the back of the Law Courts on the Strand. Run by the redoubtable Roxy Beaujolais, this is a haunt of lawyers between cases, drinking next to film posters for legal dramas like *Action for Slander* (1937). One of the few buildings that survived the Great Fire of 1666, I always seem to find myself gravitating here.

# CROWN & ANCHOR

**NEAL STREET ⊖ COVENT GARDEN**

Brewery plaques at the
Crown & Anchor

One of the pleasures of finding lettering from the past still extant in London is the reminder it transmits of long-defunct businesses and brands. The Stag Brewery in Pimlico was demolished in 1959. Undoubtedly the quality of the material used, in this case polychrome stoneware tiling, has helped preserve these brewery plaques as part of the streetscape of Covent Garden, recalling the visual splendour of the Victorian public house.

# LONDON
# RIVERSIDE

# YORK WATER GATE

**VICTORIA EMBANKMENT GARDENS ⊖ EMBANKMENT**

On John Roque's map of Georgian London, Buckingham Street is shown coming down to the River Thames from the Strand, finishing at the stairs of the York buildings, at the water's edge. The engraved lines of the rippling river can be seen lapping at an indication of steps running down into the water. Here was built an archway to provide an embarkation point from the gardens of the Duke of Buckingham's mansion, built in the same year, 1626. It was left standing when the house was demolished 50 years later, and it is still there, a wonderful showpiece for the baroque with lots of rustication and sculptured nauticalia.

This isn't a building that's been taken down piece-by-piece and removed from the river's edge to become an agreeable diversion in a public park. Here it's the river that moved. The York Water Gate is exactly where it's always been, its present position explained by Sir Joseph Bazalgette's construction of the Victoria Embankment between 1864-70, which created a new shoreline 330 feet away and housed both a new sewer and the underground railway. If one ignores the incongruous plant pots in front of it, something of its busy grandeur still remains in the shadow of the trees. One can imagine the shouts from watermen as they jostled for position, the flashing of brightly coloured silks as the Duke of Buckingham and his entourage promenaded their way onto a decorative barge.

# BATTERSEA POWER STATION

**QUEENSTOWN ROAD ⇄ BATTERSEA PARK**

The classic silhouette from Grosvenor Road on the north bank of the Thames

I once regularly saw this vast London Peculiar from a train slowing-up across the Thames as it approached Victoria station. It was always so sad to see it deteriorating from neglect, the interior torn apart and the cranes that once lifted coal from barges leaning over the water like skeletal herons. What I didn't realise was that Battersea was originally two power stations – one two-chimney structure built in the 1930s and another identical one in the '50s that gave it the fantastic four-chimney outline. The exterior was designed by Sir Giles Gilbert Scott (phone boxes, Liverpool Cathedral) and is still the largest brick structure in Europe. Since its decommissioning in 1983, successive developers have been and gone, but now it does appear to be coming back to life, albeit with the views now disturbed by the steel and glass apartments of Power Station Park. The chimneys were in such a bad state that they were taken down and rebuilt. What a temple to industry this would have made: the turbine hall once again humming with giant dynamos and lit with arcing flashes of electricity (I imagine), showing us just how awe-inspiring these powerhouses once were.

# HAMMERSMITH BRIDGE

⊖ HAMMERSMITH

**Below:** Detail of a bridge pylon decoration
**Below right:** Lyle's Golden Syrup label

This is the second bridge to stand here; the first suffered from thousands of people rushing from one side to the other during the University Boat Race, of which this is the mid-point. Bazalgette's replacement design raided the style catalogue for castles and portcullises, horses and lions, crowns and sea shells and many, many oak leaves. The real Peculiar though, for me, is that its construction (1883-7) coincides with the arrival in grocers' shops of Lyle's Golden Syrup. Surely either architect or tin designer were suddenly impressed with the other's idea of a gold and green finish. These are the original colours for the bridge, being reinstated in a 2000 renovation after an IRA bomb attack.

The bridge from the Hammersmith shore

# SOUTHERN TUNNEL HOUSE

**BLACKWALL TUNNEL APPROACH ⊖ NORTH GREENWICH**

Thomas Blashill's impressive southern gateway to the Blackwall Tunnel, 1897

In these austere days we can't imagine a building such as this being sanctioned for something as prosaic as a tunnel. But this was in the days of Victorian pride in engineering, and the Southern Tunnel House was designed by LCC architect Thomas Blashill, and completed before the tunnel was opened in 1897 by the then-Prince of Wales. Built in sandstone with numerous Art Nouveau details, there are echoes of the equally gargantuan Tower Bridge, opened three years previously.

The tunnel was desperately needed for the growing businesses and population of the east of London, and was originally just a single bore under the Thames from Greenwich to Poplar. It wasn't until 70 years later that another tunnel was opened at the side of the original, which then became just for northbound traffic.

# BLACK ROD'S STEPS

**HOUSES OF PARLIAMENT ⊖ WESTMINSTER**

The Met. keeping an eye on the Houses of Parliament

The best way to view this little pavilion is with a pair of binoculars from the other side of the Thames, or better still, from a boat. The parliamentary official Black Rod has little to do with these steps; they are named after Black Rod's Garden to which they lead, part of alterations made to the embanking wall of the Houses of Parliament in 1860. The pavilion is only a porch, so I imagine it acts as a glorified bus shelter for river passengers. Apparently, a peer getting married within the Palace of Westminster may use the steps to make good his escape (presumably with his new wife), and pupils from Westminster School row up to them once a year to partake of a cream tea on the House of Lords terrace. Police boats watch over it and all riverine activity from their station in Wapping.

# BLACKFRIARS 1864 RAILWAY BRIDGE

**BLACKFRIARS BRIDGE ⊖ BLACKFRIARS**

**Opposite:** The sheer self-confidence of a Victorian railway company. Best seen from the Thames Path on the South Bank
**Below:** Heads above water, the surviving stanchions of the original 1864 railway bridge

Protruding from the Thames next to Blackfriars railway bridge are a series of deep pink clusters of columns with foliate heads. These are the remains of another bridge on this site. Until the removal of the five latticed girders, this bridge was the oldest crossing downstream of Battersea. Joseph Cubitt and F.T. Turner built it for the London, Chatham and Dover Railway, and it is this company's insignia that forms such a show-stopping end to the series of redundant piers.

This giant badge is one of the most fabulous pieces of public heraldry in existence, and we are indeed lucky that it wasn't consigned to a scrap heap when the bridge was taken down. The integral coats-of arms are, clockwise from the top: Kent, Dover, Rochester and the City of London. The railway served most of Kent and the Channel ports and takes its motto, *Invicta*, from Kent's 'invincible' white horse. The name *Invicta* was used for the first steam locomotive to run in Kent, also becoming the first engine to travel through a railway tunnel.

LONDON CHATHAM AND DOVER RAILWAY

INVICTA

# TIDE KIOSK, WESTMINSTER BRIDGE

River Thames Tide Kiosk. The shadow is cast by the statue of *Boadicea and Her Daughters*

This must be one of the most ignored little buildings in London, as thousands of tourists pass it on their way up or down the steps from the Embankment to Westminster Bridge. There is no clue as to its use, and the tiny apertures in the sides hardly pass as windows, but inside were once automatic instruments for measuring the tides.

A contemporary account of tide gauges from the 1930s says: "A float is attached by wire via geared wheels to a recording pen which marks the tidal variations on a sheet of paper placed around a horizontal drum completely revolved every 24 hours by a clock." The gauges were checked every day, and were also used to predict tidal surges.

Obsolete now, I do hope it survives.

# OBELISK, TEDDINGTON LOCK

A Thames boundary marker on the towing path opposite Teddington

Amongst the riverside trees and undergrowth near Teddington Lock is this little obelisk on the Ham shore. It looks like a simple churchyard memorial or village market cross, but it is in fact a boundary marker denoting the extent of the jurisdiction of two river authorities. Downstream of this obelisk is the responsibility of the Port of London Authority, upstream is that of the Thames Conservancy. The difference in character is quite marked. Downstream from here the river is urbane, business-like; commerce crowding to the water's edge, the hint of ozone on the tidal mud. Upstream lies the rural Thames: overhanging trees, rowing skiffs and the ghosts of Jerome K. Jerome's *Three Men in a Boat,* trying to get to sleep under the stars.

# TRINITY BUOY WHARF
⊖ EAST INDIA

**Opposite:** Lightship LV95, built by
Philip & Son, Dartmouth, 1939
**Below:** London's only true
lighthouse, built in 1866

It needs perseverance to find this wharf, out on the Leamouth Peninsula in Orchard Place, where the River Lea does one final meander by Canning Town before reaching the Thames. Trinity House looks after our navigational warning devices and this was where they once experimented with different forms of lighthouse illumination. London's only true lighthouse was designed by Sir James Douglass in 1866 and it's here that they would have lit up the Thames with their trials of 'Argand', 'Matthew's Incandescent' and 'Hood Petroleum Vapour' burners. Equally impressive here is Lightship LV95, which served on the treacherous Goodwin Sands off the Kent coast before becoming a recording studio.

Venture up into the lighthouse now and you'll find something even odder going on. Ex-Pogue Jem Finer and Artangel, a London-based art organisation, have installed *Longplayer*: twenty minutes of sound made by Tibetan 'singing bowls', continually repeated but computer-generated so that the same sequence will not be repeated for a thousand years.

# HM VICTUALLING YARD

**GROVE STREET ⇄ DEPTFORD**

**Below:** Swords into ploughshares, cannons into bollards
**Opposite:** Gateway to the Victualling Yard in Grove Street

Many London bollards are pointed out as being recycled from old cannons, topped-out with a cannon ball in the muzzle. Well, most of them aren't, although they do take their cue from the real thing. Here, outside the 1788 gateway to what remains of the Royal Navy's Victualling Yard, are the genuine articles: an impressively heavy gun salute in Grove Street, Deptford. Strange to think that this quiet backwater was once a noisy bustling hive of activity, the Victualling Yard being used for the storage of provisions and clothing; all the essentials for an eighteenth-century navy.

THE PASSAGE OF THE
TUNNEL LIES BETWEEN
THE 1908 RAILWAY BRIDGE
AND THE MODERNIST
TWICKENHAM ROAD
BRIDGE.

# FOOT TUNNEL ENTRANCES, RICHMOND & ST. MARGARETS

≥ RICHMOND

**Opposite top:** Richmond shore entrance
**Opposite bottom:** St. Margarets shore entrance
**Below:** The tunnel runs approximately along the bottom of the photograph

Twickenham Bridge was only built in 1933, as all attempts to cross the river by road at this point had been thwarted because any approach to it would mean cutting through the Old Deer Park. But there was a foot tunnel, and the Richmond shore entrance remains clearly visible *(opposite)*. Someone who works on the river told me that it's still possible to crawl through it, but the thought sends shivers down my spine as assiduously as drips of ice cold water would run down one's neck in the darkness. This curious pepperpot building is carefully built in brick with a tiled roof and a little metal ventilator on top, like a tiny castle turret. This heavily-secured, green-painted door is set in a Gothic arch and hung with a pair of seductively curved wrought-iron hinges.

On the opposite bank sits its companion, even more alone, identical in all ways except that there's more fencing to stop you getting near it. The passage of the tunnel lies between the 1908 railway bridge, where trains thunder over the houseboats on its open steel spandrels, and the modernist Twickenham road bridge from which the pictures on this page were taken.

# LONDON
# VENTILATING

# TOWER BRIDGE CHIMNEY

**Previous spread:** Gibson Square pavilion. See page 114
**Below:** Guardroom Chimney on Tower Bridge (west side)

There is so much to marvel at here on London's landmark bridge. A Gothic fairytale designed by Sir Horace Jones to chime with the Tower of London next door, this combined bascule and suspension bridge uniquely captures the imagination of Londoners and tourists alike. But how many give even a first glance at this little cast-iron fixture on the western balustrade of the northern approach? It looks very much like one of the lamp standards without the light, but it is, in fact, a chimney that once serviced a fireplace far below, which warmed a guardroom used by officials from the Tower. The ironfounder's name and address is still perfectly visible on the flue: Durham Brothers, 205 Bow Road E.

# SEWER VENTILATING LAMP

**CARTING LANE ⊖ CHARING CROSS**

Sewer Ventilator on Carting Lane, off the Strand

Geoffery Fletcher, in *The London Nobody Knows*, says of this curiosity at the side of the Savoy Hotel "...I often tremble for its future." That was in 1962, and I cheered to myself as it became immediately apparent that not only had the Patent Sewer Ventilating Lamp survived, but it was glowing greenly with gas. Whether it was running on excess gas from the sewers was uncertain, but if not then somebody needs to be applauded for saving this Peculiar and connecting it up to the mains.

The column is hollow, designed to allow sewer vapours to ascend to the lantern where they could be safely burnt off, conveniently lighting the street at the same time. A great example of Victorian recycling.

# O2 ARENA CHIMNEY

◉ NORTH GREENWICH

Blackwall Tunnel Ventilator inside the
O2 Arena

If you look at a street map of London you'll notice that the south-bound Blackwall Tunnel (separated from its northbound counterpart by about an eighth of a mile) is only under the Thames for less than half its overall length. As it reaches the southern shore it needs to do a sharp right-hander in order to run down the Greenwich Peninsula (marketing-speak for Bugsby's Marshes).

It's still a quarter of a mile from fresh air so there has to be a ventilator, coincidentally where they decided to build The Dome. So that big depression on its south-west corner is to accommodate a white chimney that releases traffic exhaust out over the Millennium Greenwich Village.

# GRACECHURCH STREET BOLLARD

Ventilator as bollard, Gracechurch Street

This piece of classic City of London street-hardware is painted in what are almost the 'corporate colours' for this kind of thing, perhaps taking a cue from the black-and-white striping used during wartime blackout conditions for hazard warnings in the darkened streets.

This proud chap sits on a tiny traffic island where Gracechurch Street meets Eastcheap, surrounded by plainer fellows and topped off with a giant lemon squeezer. I am reliably informed by a drain savant that it is simply a bollard that doubles up as a ventilator for the lavatories next door, behind those blue railings.

# GIBSON SQUARE, ISLINGTON

⊖ ANGEL

A classical park pavilion does not seem like a remarkable sight amongst the lawns and roses of Gibson Square. But the dome in this case is an open mesh, for this is a ventilator shaft terminal for the Victoria Line rumbling underneath. The architect was Quinlan Terry, who I think argues that the classical orders of architecture were handed down by God, perhaps as an appendix to the Ten Commandments. He is seen as very controversial, precisely because his work is so uncontroversial. But who couldn't admire the level of thought and principles that he poured into an otherwise mundane tunnel ventilator?

Terry is also an architectural rarity himself – he can draw supremely well, and his practice with fellow classicist Raymond Erith produced beautiful pieces of artwork to demonstrate their buildings. He naturally called this 1969 ventilator the Tower of the Winds.

# LONDON
# MISCELLANY

# THE ROUTEMASTER BUS

**TOWER HIIL/TRAFALGAR SQUARE. BUS ROUTE 15 (HERITAGE)**

The Routemaster was born out of the need to replace London's trolleybuses, and the result, after two years of harsh testing, drove onto the capital's streets in 1959, the same year as the Mini. And it's just as much of a design classic. The design brief was as it should be, to build a bus that was right from everybody's point of view: the operating managers, the drivers and, of course, the passengers. Weight reduction came with its aluminium body, styled by Douglas Scott; retaining the isolated driving position meant better visibility and no distraction from passengers; and comfort came with independent front suspension, shock absorbers and warm-air heating, features hitherto only found on cars.

2,760 had been made by 1968, and passengers, drivers and conductors all loved them. And still do. After being threatened with extinction for so long, the bus was finally withdrawn at the end of 2005, with a few kept for a heritage route. There is now a new 'Routemaster', inspired by the original, but that name should only be used for what was one of the most remarkable vehicles to have ever served London.

# ARCHWAY BRIDGE

**ARCHWAY ROAD, HIGHGATE ⊖ ARCHWAY**

Below and following spread:
Imagine walking along a quiet
suburban street and suddenly looking
down from this

By the early nineteenth century, the dramatic increase in road traffic necessitated a route in and out of London that would bypass Highgate Hill, particularly in foul weather. Amazingly, a tunnel was tried first, but this was quickly followed by Archway Road, cut through in 1812. The first bridge to carry the road over the ravine was an aqueduct-style affair by John Nash, replaced in 1897 by this elaborate cast-iron arch, designed by Alexander Binnio.

Its sinister silhouette, high above the carriageway as you climb up from Upper Holloway, never fails to darken my mood. Suicides were once common here, with bodies falling like rag dolls from the parapet. One can only start to imagine the misery in those last footsteps that tapped along Hornsey Lane, followed by a leap into oblivion.

# GRAIN SILO

**NORTH WOOLWICH ROAD ⊖ PONTOON DOCK**

When I was a small child in the '50s, I vividly remember being taken on a boat trip downstream on the River Thames. In particular, I recall seeing the seemingly endless docks and wharves, the tall cranes swinging cargo up from the holds of steamships and the men shouting to each other from high up on the wooden ledges of warehouse openings. It was a world of intense activity and excitement, noisy with the blasts of boat horns and the constant clanking of chains. Black tugs with red funnels fussed in and out of billows of white steam, and I felt a little frightened to see things so foreign to my rural sensibilities.

Most of it has now disappeared. Containerisation meant that the traditional dockers and their swinging cranes were no longer needed. Their docks became scenes of dereliction, divided up by vast and empty sheets of water. Until, of course, the chancers and developers moved in, making lunchtime presentations on their gin-fuelled motor yachts.

In amongst the screensaved office hierarchies and bleak 'lifestyle' apartments, there lurks the odd reminder of the original dockland industries. Out in North Woolwich, the Royal Victoria Dock was home to Spiller's Millennium Mills, which supplied flour to the ever-increasing London market, and on the Pontoon Dock a row of grain elevators pumped imported grain from the bowels of ships. All has now been sterilised; 'corporate hospitality functions' are reached via roads lined with maintenance-free shrubs set in bark chippings. But there is one survivor from the Pontoon Dock, peering over the trees and gardens like a lost, white-shrouded giant. Just one grain silo, signed with a letter 'D' to guide its next cargo to the correct berth. A cargo that may prove to be somewhat elusive.

# MERIDIAN STUDS

**PARK VISTA, GREENWICH ⮀ MAZE HILL**

**Opposite:** East meets West in Park Vista and Feathers Place

The longitude zero degree meridian line is made much of in Greenwich. Up at the Royal Observatory on the hill there are brass rules, aligned telescopes and a time ball, and out across the country are markers that keep the faith. And, near to its birthplace, is this row of studs across a back street in Greenwich.

I once walked down Feathers Place, the road you can see in the background, and saw a 'For Sale' notice outside a house that appeared to be bisected by the meridian, so I rang for details from the estate agent. Of course they went on at great length about the fact that the front living room was west of the line, while the dining room and kitchen was east. I think this Amazing Fact resulted in a few bob being eased onto the sale price.

# CROCKER'S FOLLY

**ABERDEEN PLACE ⬌ WARWICK AVENUE**

In the late 1890s, construction was underway on the last few miles of the Great Central Railway into London. Somebody told Frank Crocker that the new terminus would be somewhere near here, in quiet Aberdeen Place in Lisson Grove. So on the appropriate corner he built his railway hotel in 1898, a big airy hostelry that utilised everything out of the style catalogue: shaped brickwork, ashlar stone, white-plastered Moorish windows, marble bars, engraved glass and mahoghany fixtures.

The railway, of course, failed to turn towards Aberdeen Place, but carried on for another three quarters of a mile into Marylebone. Crocker, now ruined, apparently took his own life by jumping from an upper storey window.

# CAB SHELTERS

FOR EXAMPLE: ⊖ WARWICK AVENUE, TEMPLE

**Opposite:** Warwick Avenue cab shelter, by the entrance to the Underground station
**Below:** Cabbie at Warwick Avenue

We so very nearly lost these curious structures from the London streetscape. They were the result of a rare philanthropic gesture by a newpaper editor in 1875, when Sir George Armstrong of *The Globe* founded The Cabmen's Shelter Fund with the Earl of Shaftesbury as its president. The initials 'CSF' can clearly be seen amongst the fretwork decorations under the eaves. The idea was to provide cabmen with a refuge where they could "obtain good and wholesome refreshment at very moderate prices". As alcohol wasn't served, there was the added benefit that your cabbie might be sober. As they appeared in the horse-drawn age, the Metropolitan Police agreed to their erection on the streets provided they took up no more space than a horse and cab.

Sixty-one shelters were built, costing about £200 each. Thirteen still exist, including these examples by Warwick Avenue Underground station and in Temple Place: identical kit-form structures with timber-framed walls, tongue and groove panels, a felt-clad roof lined-out with terracotta ridge tiles and a little lead-capped ventilation cupola. The CSF still exists and the shelters are now Grade II listed, with a number of bodies helping with their restoration and maintenance.

I was made very welcome inside the Warwick Avenue shelter, where everything is designed to maximise on the limited interior. I particularly liked the range of sauces available and the microwave oven slung up out of harm's way like a hotel bedroom TV, (for which I did at first mistake it).

# TRAFALGAR SQUARE EX-POLICE POST

**Opposite:** The pigeon-haunted kiosk on the south-east corner of Trafalgar Square
**Below:** The blue police post in Eastcheap, now removed

Auxiliary police stations have all but disappeared from the London scene. Once, the Metropolitan copper on the beat kept in touch with his nick from strategically-placed miniature offices. The police box crowned with its flashing blue light is still familiar to us, but only because it's the transport-of-choice for Doctor Who.

The evidence can still be found of some of these outposts, and here in the south-east corner of Trafalgar Square is a particularly well-disguised example. Its interior is inside one of four lamp pillars that sit at the extremities of the square. There's just about room for an averaged-sized policeman and his truncheon, but on my visit I was disappointed to find the lantern base now functions as a refuge for the Square's cleaners and their newspapers. The polygonal bronze lantern is not, as London myth would have it, one of a series taken from Nelson's flagship HMS *Victory*, but the panopticon design is unique to the lamps in the square, believed by its designer to provide, like a diamond, more light from its multiple refraction.

Once upon a time in Eastcheap there stood a perfect example of a simple column that once held a telephone for use by constables on their beats in the City of London (left). An incoming call set the little light flashing on and off to alert them. Sadly, it was removed and all that was left was a little patch of tarmac on the pavement. I wonder why it couldn't have been left there; even if it was no longer required for police duties, its purpose could have been set out on a little plaque for the future education of those who grew up without these unassuming but bright little pieces of street furniture.

# LEINSTER GARDENS

**Opposite:** 23-24 Leinster Gardens, the houses that are all front

The postman knocks in vain at the doors of 23-24 Leinster Gardens, where the glass and woodwork of sightless windows are only grey and white paint. No twitching curtains, no lamps lit at dusk – what you see here is literally all there is.

In the late 1860s, the Metropolitan Railway extended their operations west from Edgware Road to Gloucester Road. Early underground railway engineering was 'cut-and-cover', which meant that instead of deep tube tunnelling, cuttings were excavated at the surface and then covered over. This method facilitated a wider, airier environment, essential when the locomotive power was still steam engines. So the Metropolitan cut and covered its way through the quiet streets of Paddington and Bayswater, fully expecting to pull down a section of stuccoed terrace in Leinster Gardens. But the locals were enraged that their street should suffer such an indignity and demanded that the frontages of the houses concerned should be retained, keeping up appearances at street level.

So now the trains serving the District and Circle Lines trundle underneath, their passengers unaware of the film set above their heads. Up in Leinster Gardens, one of the two hotels next door joins in on the fun by extending their balcony flowers in front of the neighbouring *trompe l'œil* windows. Probationers at Paddington Green Police Station are allegedly sent round to them in order to conduct spurious enquiries, whilst presumably senior officers hide around the corner sniggering.

# PORTERS' REST

**PICCADILLY ⊖ HYDE PARK CORNER**

This curious item of street furniture is on the south side of Piccadilly where the slip road debouches onto Hyde Park Corner, just before the underpass. It is the only surviving example of a porters' rest that I know of and its preservation is remarkable. Before mechanised transport, goods were carried on pack mules and horse-drawn wagons, but equally large loads would be carried on the bent backs of men. This wooden shelf, supported on two cast-iron pillars, is positioned at exactly the right height for a porter to turn and rest his pack without taking it off his back.

By the mid-nineteenth century these conveniences were fast disappearing, and in 1861 the MP for Shrewsbury, RL Slaney, suggested that "...this porters' rest be erected...by the Vestry of St. George, Hanover Square for the benefit of porters and others carrying burdens, as a relic of a past world in London's history....It is hoped that the people will aid its preservation". Today it is more likely to be the resting place for a hot styrene coffee cup than a colporteur's pack of bibles, but it is nevertheless still a welcome addition in the busy Piccadilly streetscape.

# CORAM FIELDS

**GUILFORD STREET ⊖ RUSSELL SQUARE**

**Opposite and below:** Leave your unwanted infants here. The Coram Fields baby niche

Nobody cared much for illigitimate babies in the eighteenth century, particularly if they were poor, and their pale corpses were often discarded like so much unwanted refuse on rubbish tips, or even dumped at the side of the road. This appalling state of affairs did not go unnoticed, however, and a glimmer of hope for foundlings came with the red-coated Captain Thomas Coram, who was determined to build a Foundling Hospital.

George II was moved enough to sign a charter, Handel gave his fees from performances of *Messiah* and Hogarth designed a letterhead for Coram's fundraiser. In 1740, the hospital's committee voted that 60 children be immediately offered places in the new building to be erected here in Holborn.

Coram's hospital was demolished in 1926, the empty space now, ironically, a park where adults must be accompanied by a child. Almost all that survives, of the exterior at least, is a range of little buildings along what is now Guilford Street, including this stone niche where desperate mothers could leave their unwanted or unsustainable babies. On the opening day of 2 June, 1756, 117 wriggling infants were left in this alcove. By the end of March 1760, no fewer than 14,934 babies had been abandoned here.

# ARP STRETCHER RAILINGS

FOR EXAMPLE: TABARD STREET ⊖ BOROUGH

**Opposite & below:** The now removed stretcher railings in Harleyford Street, Oval
**Bottom:** An ARP Warden's badge

The ARP (Air Raid Precautions) first aiders were called 'stretcher parties' in the London Blitz. On hand as soon as the All Clear had sounded from the rooftop sirens, they became the frontline in treating the injured after bombing raids on the capital. In *Wartime: Britain 1939–1945*, Juliet Gardiner writes that they "would arrive to treat minor injuries on the spot and gently lift the more seriously injured on to stretchers – or a door or plank if no stretchers were available – and into vehicles". Britain was generally ill-prepared for the Second World War, but plans for dealing with the aftermath of devastating air raids quickly saw stores filling up with metal stretchers and tens of thousands of papier-mâché coffins, most of which, surprisingly, were not required. The biggest problem was that large sections of the population were rendered homeless.

Inevitably, the late 1940s saw a huge demand for housing in the battered, war-torn capital, and planners became very excited at the possibilities for urban renewal. But amongst all the drawing up of elevations, quantity surveying and sifting through fixtures and fittings catalogues, I wonder who first turned an ARP stretcher on its side and thought: "Hmm, this would make a good council flat railing…"? Certainly there was a readily available supply, so brick piers were designed to take them. So preposterous was the idea of such a purposeful object being so imaginatively recycled that they quickly achieved urban-mythic status. When I first saw these prime examples in Harleyford Street, opposite the Oval cricket ground, I must admit I did have a slight moment of doubt. Until I noticed the four little kinks in the supporting tubes: a simple utilitarian device to keep the stretcher off the ground or the floor of an ambulance.

The Harleyford Street examples were the best that I found, but the local council decided to replace them with the usual straightforward railings because of degradation. The Stretcher Railing Society aims to preserve as many as possible, and more examples can be seen in Tabard Street.

# CARSHALTON PONDS BUS STOP HOLES

**NORTH STREET, CARSHALTON ⇌ CARSHALTON**

Quite recently I came across a very peculiar Peculiar, in time for it to round off this exploration of London's curiosities.

It's a brick wall near Carshalton Ponds in North Street, with a short section displaying these holes, gouged out of what must be relatively soft brick. I pondered them for some time, and on turning round saw that they were immediately opposite a bus stop. The thought occurred that these holes had been made by schoolchildren as they waited for their bus, religiously winding an old penny (probably their bus fare) to create a cavity. Some are mere initial scourings, others the fruit of prolonged labour. I have yet to find a softish brick, and indeed a suitably old penny, to see if this premise is correct. It would take time, as these holes must have been made over a considerable period. My researches have all drawn blanks, so my last attempt will be to find a Carshalton pensioner who will finally admit to his early preoccupation with coins and bricks.

And so, we come to the end. For now, at least. There will always be something slightly odd out of the corner of the eye, some forgotten curiosity that suddenly makes an appearance, or even a brand new Peculiar that makes us say once again:

"I wonder what that is?"

# FURTHER READING

Below is a selection of books that I have found very helpful in my research and deliberations. Many will unfortunately be out-of-print, but all are worth seeking out.

*A to Z of Georgian London, The* London Topographical Society 1982

*Buildings of England Series, London Volumes* Niklaus Pevsner & others, Penguin and Yale

*Changing Metropolis, The* Gavin Stamp, Viking 1984

*Guide to the Architecture of London, A* Edward Jones & Christopher Woodward, Weidenfeld & Nicolson 1983

*Highgate Cemetery* John Gay & Felix Barker, John Murray 1988

*Lights Out for the Territory* Iain Sinclair, Granta 1997

*London Explorer* Peter Jackson & W. Crawford Snowden, Associated Newspapers 1953

*London is Stranger than Fiction* Peter Jackson, Associated Newspapers 1951

*London Nobody Knows, The* Geoffrey Fletcher, Hutchinson 1962

*London Orbital* Iain Sinclair, Penguin 2003

*London Sight Unseen* Snowdon & Gwyn Headley, Weidenfeld & Nicolson 1999

*London Under London* Richard Trench & Ellis Hillman, John Murray 1984

*Nairn's London* Ian Nairn, Penguin 1966

*Other London* Paul Barkshire, Lennard Publishing 1989

*Unexplored London* Paul Barkshire, Lennard Publishing 1987

*Wartime: Britain 1939-1945* Juliet Gardiner, Headline 2004

*World for a Shilling, The* Michael Leapman, Review 2002

# ACKNOWLEDGEMENTS

George Ashley
Wilfred Ashley
Bates of Jermyn Street
Berry Bros & Rudd
Stephen Farrow
Amy Kennington at Pulse Creative
Bryn Porter
St. Mary Rotherhithe
Rosemarie Shaw
Iain Sinclair
James Smith

Michele Turriani at Trinity Buoy Wharf
Tom Wareham
Philip Wilkinson

Design concept: Webb & Webb Design Ltd

Temple Bar photograph on page 60 courtesy Historic England Archive
Photograph of trains on page 107 © Wilfred Ashley

**Opposite:** The Jerusalem Tavern, a favourite Peculiar amongst public houses. There's nowhere quite like it in London. 55 Britton Street, Clerkenwell ⊖ Farringdon

© Peter Ashley 2019
World copyright reserved

ISBN: 978 1 85149 918 2

First published by ACC Art Books in 2019
Reprinted 2023

British Library Cataloguing-in-Publication Data
A catalogue record for this book is available from the British
Library.

The author and publisher gratefully acknowledge the permission
granted to reproduce the copyright material in this book. Every
effort has been made to trace copyright holders and to obtain
their permission for the use of copyright material. The publisher
apologises for any errors or omissions in the text and would be
grateful if notified of any corrections that should be incorporated
in future reprints or editions of this book.

Design concept: Webb & Webb Design Ltd.

Front Cover: The author's dog-eared and appropriately out-of-
date London Street Atlas.
Frontispiece: Battersea Power Station (see page 94).

Printed in China
for ACC Art Books Ltd., Woodbridge, Suffolk, UK

www.accartbooks.com